# ReInventing Positivity

## Power To Embrace Negativity, Create Positivity And Live Your Happiest Life

DR. TERESA RENFROE

*"If I have the belief that I can do it, I shall surely acquire the capacity to do it even if I may not have it at the beginning." -Mahatma Gandhi*

Copyright © 2022 by Dr. Teresa Renfroe

All rights reserved. No part of this publication may be reproduced, distributed, or transmitted in any form or by any means, without prior written permission.

**Published in the United States by Paper Owl Publishing in**

**Sarasota, FL 34233**

Disclaimer: The information presented is the author's opinion and does not constitute any health or medical advice. The content of this book is for informational purposes only and is not intended to diagnose, treat, cure, or prevent any condition or disease. Please seek advice from your healthcare provider for your health concerns prior to taking healthcare advice from this book.

This book is designed to provide information regarding the subject matter covered, negativity bias, and thinking positively. By its sale, neither the publisher nor the author is engaged in rendering medical or professional services. If expert assistance or counseling is needed, the services of a competent professional should be sought.

The publisher and the author make no guarantees concerning the level of success you may experience by following the advice and strategies contained in this book, and you accept the risk that results will differ for each individual.

**Reinventing Positivity/Dr. Teresa Renfroe**. -- 1st ed.

Cover Design by Dr. Teresa Renfroe

# CONTENTS

Preface .................................................................... 8

Acknowledgments ................................................ 11

Introduction.......................................................... 12

Part 1

INTERPRETATION ................................................ 22

1

My Journey Through Negativity ............................ 23

Part 2

THE SCIENCE ..................................................... 30

2

Discovery of Negativity in Epigenetics ..................... 31

3

The Negativity Bias .................................................. 34

4

Negativity and Cellular Aging.................................. 42

5

Positivity "Matters" .................................................. 47

6

Yin & Yang .................................................................. 52

Part 3

LIVING LIFE ............................................................... 58

7

Terminal Cancer Diagnosis.......................................... 59

Part 4

THE PRACTICE .......................................................... 64

8

Glass Half Empty ........................................................ 65

9

The PAACT Program .................................................. 69

10

Social Connections....................................................... 78

11

SUCCESS .................................................................... 84

12

THE PAACT PROGRAM ........................................... 89

JOURNAL PAGES

References ................................................................ 114
About the Author ...................................................... 118

# **Preface**

I have always been a person who thinks ahead and is prepared. I was the kid who picked out their clothes the night before and made sure I was never late to school by being super early. That's right, I'm the person who always shows up early for an appointment and waits patiently. I never mind waiting, probably because I spend a lot of time in my head preparing for my next future event. You have to laugh at that one. I always have an umbrella in the car, I take a jacket to dinner and the movies and if I want to make sure I don't forget an important paper or something I have to take with me, I put it on the floor by the front door so that I have to pick it up on my way out.

I have been doing this preparing for the future ever since I was a kid. I play the "what if" game. What if it's freezing in the theater? What if I'm late to work? Again, I always have a jacket handy and I leave super early and make sure I'm never late. This game of "what if" goes deeper than just going out to the movies or getting to work on time. Ruminating can become a beacon of negative reeling thoughts that can take you spiraling out of control. It can distort your view, make you anxious and stressed, and does nothing to help you achieve success or create happiness.

This book will take you through real-life events that will help you understand more about being aware of your negative thoughts and how to embrace them instead of trying to shove them in a corner. I have compiled research on negativity bias to give you insight into why humans are innately negative. Even though it's built into our DNA, it doesn't mean that we can't be aware of it, accept it and make changes that fill our lives with more joy.

I developed the PAACT Program which incorporates 5 elements:

- Perspective
- Awareness
- Acceptance
- Change
- Time

The PAACT Program implements simple steps that show you how to see a negative situation, by looking at the perspective, becoming aware of your thoughts, accepting the thoughts, implementing change, and allowing time to rewire your brain.

Over time, this method boosts positivity, and gratefulness, and rewires the brain to optimize performance and allow natural processes to take place so that you can live healthier, happier, and richer lives.

# Acknowledgments

I have to start by thanking my wonderful partner in life, Jessica, for allowing me the time I needed to finally complete this book, for always encouraging me, and for staying by my side through my cancer treatments and rough times. You are amazing, and I love you.

I would also like to thank my Mother for listening and always being there for me, loving me unconditionally, and helping me through some very tough times. I thank my Father and stepmother for never giving up on me and continuing to love me no matter what and for coming to my bedside during my cancer surgery. You are all phenomenal and I love you.

I couldn't have done this without your love and support, so to you all, I dedicate this book.

# Introduction

I spent a lot of time wondering why I was so negative all the time. Mostly because I lived with someone that kept telling me I was being negative. I kept being asked if I realized that I was dwelling on things that hadn't happened yet and I was being told over and over again to try to be positive.

This nagging about my so-called negativeness, over time, began to make me question if I was happy. I of course equated being negative with not being happy, but I WAS happy. I am naturally a happy person. I just always like to be prepared and I think that can sometimes come across negatively. There have been many times when life was hard and I was emotional about it, but that doesn't mean I'm not a happy person. It's just life, c'est la vie.

I started realizing that many people were just as negative as I was at the time but I guess when you live with someone that is ruminating and dwelling on things it can saturate your daily life and create negativity. So instead of pointing out the other person's flaws, I began to pay attention to myself and practiced becoming mindful of the times when I was being negative.

One day, the realization hit me smack in the face, that my nature was to always be thinking ahead and contemplating what could happen next, which didn't seem negative to me. I just like to be prepared. That's not such a bad thing. I tried many times to stop and live in the moment. BE HERE NOW! Stop dwelling on the future! Nonetheless, I found it very hard to do. Being prepared for the future is a very natural and unintentional way of thinking. I say unintentionally because I wasn't purposefully trying to be negative. It was natural and automatic. I would analyze myself as any good doctor would, but the fact is that I am truly happy. I just tend to question life with "what if?".

At one point my boss lost his job and then I began thinking "What if I lose my job?". Seems normal to me when you work with someone for a while and don't see them doing anything wrong and then the hammer comes down and they get fired, that you might have a natural fear that your head is next. My problem was that I didn't stop at losing the job, my mind would spiral into a sequence of reeling thoughts that if I lost my job, I would lose my house and my car, and on and on, and then what would I do?

This domino effect of questioning the future because my boss lost his job had nothing to do with me, but it made me uncomfortable and have fear based on the circumstances. It's fear of the unknown that keeps us dwelling on the future of events that haven't taken place. In some way, if you stop and look at that energetically, it's sending out negativity constantly. Or is it?

It seems so natural to go down these paths to prepare for the worst but not only is that not healthy but do you think I expected to get a positive outcome from that negativity? No, at that time I wasn't. I wasn't seeing the positive outcome of the negative situation and I was reeling and dwelling on something that more than likely wasn't going to happen. I won't say that there wasn't a possibility that I would get fired too, but there were no signs at that time that my head was on the chopping block along with my boss. That kind of thought process does allow you the opportunity to make plans. So in some way, there is a small positive outcome to the negativity. The point here is that it isn't natural to try and control your thoughts to always be positive.

To me, it has become a conventional misunderstanding. You can practice not being negative or practice always being positive but again it's not realistic that it won't happen again. So why not embrace the negative and find the positive within it? This is a much better exercise in human motivation. Millions of people everyday use self-help gurus to try and stay positive, but the universe was born out of light and dark, yin and yang, so positivity and negativity must coexist. Don't worry, I will help you understand more about the yin and yang theory later in Chapter 6, so let's continue our introduction.

Speaking of being positive, I have always enjoyed motivational speakers. That's right! I'm not dissing affirmations or going to motivational conferences and retreats. I think it's great to expand your horizons but there has to be a balance and I will show you later why it's okay to have negative thoughts and how to use them to project positivity. I like the idea of thinking positively, setting goals, and being successful.

I have read great motivators like Louise Hay, Tony Robbins, Eckhart Tolle, Thich Nhat Hanh, and Pema Chodron and practiced removing negative obstacles, saying affirmations, creating vision boards, and visualizing growth and positivity for the future. And yet still to this day even though I am very happy and have used all of these great techniques, I tend to come up with negative circumstances and create negative scenarios. That which goes up must come down so for every negative there must be a positive, remember our yin and yang theory?

Ok, so let's be real, it's a natural part of human beings to be negative. There's a well-known phenomenon that everything is in flux, and according to Heraclitus, everything is constantly changing. This flux is also a natural occurrence as the day moves into night and night into day, how fall becomes winter and winter becomes spring. This is another example of our theory of Yin and Yang.

Life is made up of just as much negative as it is positive. A good example of this is a bright sunny Florida day that in a few hours turns negative after a Cat 4 hurricane comes barreling through. But then we always look on the bright side as the sun begins to shine and the community comes together to help each other to overcome devastation and loss. Nature shows us how positivity and negativity work daily, we just have to pay attention. Science has proven a negative cognitive bias, we call it the negativity bias.

I see this negativity bias every day in my work. Of course, I work in the medical field so it's not always a happy environment but it's the little things that I notice people can be negative about. In my job, I have to ask patients for their insurance cards every time I see them because I have to scan them into the system. It's a hospital policy for the clinic that I coordinate and to me not a big deal. I would say 7 out of 10 people have some snide remark about how they have been here before, and they have been coming to this hospital forever, and that all their information should be in the system and they don't understand why we have to do this every time. You can hear the negativity droning on and on. Well, all those things are probably true but I have to adhere to policy and I wouldn't ask if I didn't need the card.

That very statement is the point of this if I didn't need to scan the card as a part of my job, then why in the world would I go out of my way to ask them for it, wait for them to find it and then go through the motions of scanning it. I think most people are not going to waste time doing unnecessary tasks at work, especially if it means pissing off a patient. Every single time I tell them the same thing, that it's a policy and I apologize for the inconvenience. I shouldn't have to apologize, but I am polite and patient.

It's ridiculous that people get upset over something as menial as being asked to get out an insurance card. It's not that difficult to do and they have to sit and wait anyway, so they might as well be compliant and do it with a smile on their faces. I enjoy my work and I don't let their protesting get to me. I take their negativity and turn it into a smile, a kind, and sincere voice, and a thank you.

During my teaching days as a professor and administrator at a local acupuncture college in Sarasota

Florida, one class I taught was the practice management class to the graduating students. In this class I had the graduates create a vision board that incorporated not only their vision for their medical practices in acupuncture, but also their general finances, health, family, lifestyle, and any other areas of life they wanted to flourish in. I always received good feedback from this exercise because a lot of students felt like they were able to "get in touch" with a side of themselves they had been missing for the three years they had been in school. The students didn't realize how much they had left behind certain aspects of their lives during their schooling. I loved hearing about their positive projections and desires for opening an acupuncture practice and getting their lives back on track. I reminded them that putting out that positive energy would motivate them to be successful and accomplish many of their desires in life, and bring to fruition the vision board they had created.

There was of course some negative energy also from the students. Semester after semester I would listen to all the negative thoughts students had about how hard it was for some of them to keep moving forward and how they were afraid they wouldn't pass the boards. The list goes on and on. As a professor and later as an academic dean, I always tried to be encouraging and would counsel students and help them by being a mentor.

I started thinking about negativity and its relationship to positivity. Especially looking at it from a Chinese medicine perspective. Sometimes it felt like the negativity overshadowed the positivity. Partly the students were exhausted from the rigorous and intensive five-year Master's degree program they spent three years completing and a lot of them had financial difficulties. It became harder and harder for some of the students to work full-time and pull off this intensive coursework. The positive note was graduating and seeing a light at the end of the tunnel, knowing they would soon take boards and become physicians. Now that's a pretty positive outcome! I saw a little of myself in them and it made me think even more about why people in general tend to be so negative. Those moments with my students sparked the idea for this book.

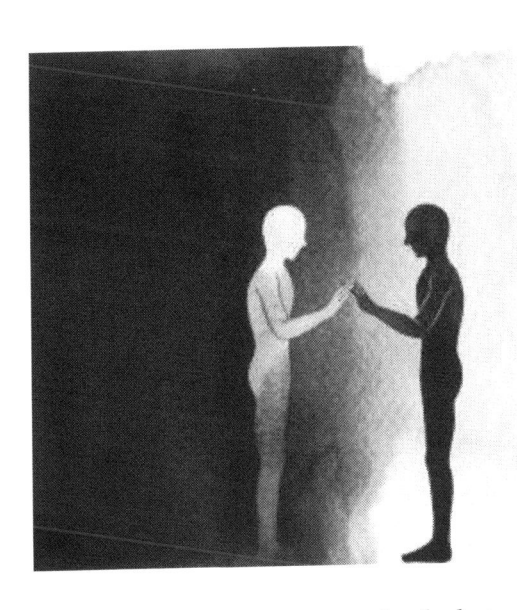

*"All we are is a result of what we have thought." - Buddha*

# Part 1

## INTERPRETATION

# 1

## My Journey Through Negativity

I spent many years diving deep into my inner consciousness, contemplating and reflecting on my negative thoughts and my happiness. I knew that I tended to relish in the thoughts of the future, which came out as negative energy to some of the people around me. Mostly fear-based thoughts like when I lost my job in 2008 and the stock market crashed and I had to take unemployment. The fear of being unable to pay my rent and all my other bills was a real downer that created a lot of stress for me and unwanted stress for others. This real-life scenario is a common factor all over the world for a lot of people, but there is always a positive side and that is what we have to get in tune with. How do we look at negativity and see the positive side, especially in times when we feel devastated? This can be difficult since our emotions of sadness, anger, and resentment usually take over and we become blind to the possibilities of any positive outcome.

Like I said before, I'm not a negative person, not in the least I love spontaneously being goofy. I might walk past someone's office at work and break into some crazy ridiculous dance move just to be funny. Not a single person has ever NOT laughed. Still, the realization that as happy as I am, this negativity at the time was putting a damper on my relationship. Interestingly, other people don't realize they have the same negative thought processes. Maybe they aren't aware of it or they aren't being criticized for it. My continued self-awareness helped me begin my journey through negativity or should I say my journey through awareness of the positive.

My negative thoughts about my boss being let go and allowing it to affect me led me down a path of thinking that I would lose so much more than my job. My boss getting let go had nothing to do with me, so why did I go down that path? I was continually looking at the possibility that something bad might happen and living in the "what if" moment.

Living in the "what if" can make you miserable when you're trying to have fun. Here's an example of a "what if" moment and how it can put a damper on a great day. You're going zip-lining and thinking what if the line breaks? You decide to tell your friend that's out to have fun with you that you are nervous the line will break and you aren't sure you want to go through with it. Meanwhile, you just paid good money to do this and you are holding up the line of people who are anxious to go. That can put a real downer on your fun and create unwanted stress for you and your friend. Another example is you are going on a hike and thinking what if I get lost, which did happen to me once but I found my way, so as you can see it's kind of ridiculous to put that energy into the "what if" since you have to deal with the problem head-on if it were to happen anyway.

Let me put this into another perspective, you can carry a map and a cell phone or any other tools to prepare for your hike but if you are zip lining and it breaks you just have to deal with the consequences. Bad things do happen and are always possible but generating that negative thought process can take the fun out of life.

When life throws you lemons you have to make lemonade, as the saying goes. We can spend our whole lives in the "what if" moment, but trying to move forward and be more positive is sometimes easier said than done.

Some people can be more negative by mimicking others who are negative, though I'm not so sure this is necessarily true. For instance, being brought up in a family that tends to be more negative or hanging around with friends that project bitterness and despair might make someone a little more negative. We can imagine that this could be a learned response, that having negative family members would automatically make you as negative as they are.

It makes sense that children are influenced in some ways by their parents and their surroundings, but science says it's deeper than that. My search for understanding this innate response to life opened many doors to the possibility that it's just as natural for us to be negative as it is for us to be positive.

It isn't just situations of ruminating on the future that creates negativity, it's also actions like gossiping, bad-mouthing others, and spewing anger and hatred. These actions create stress around us, cause health problems, and are bad for self-confidence and karma. That's right no matter your spirituality, you reap what you sow. If you set a path for yourself to spread negativity then you cannot expect anything back from life but negativity.

I know it's an oxymoron to be positively negative but if I look at myself as someone who can do anything I put my mind to and believe that I can achieve greatness and be successful, then how is it that I can find the negative in just about anything? Why does this happen and where does it come from?

It turns out that humans are hardwired for negativity and we are predisposed genetically through our DNA. This might seem surprising but there's a lot of proof in the pudding. Scientists are discovering this negative phenomenon in epigenetics, the study of how our behaviors and environment can cause changes that affect the way our genes work. And yes, our genes affect our thinking, behavior, and consciousness.

Through the years I knew there had to be answers to this phenomenon and I learned how to take my perceived negativity and turn it into positivity using a program I developed called the PAACT Program. PAACT stands for perspective, awareness, acceptance, change, and time, and I will cover this program in Part 4 of *The Practice* section of this book.

*"Change the way you look at things and the things you look at change."*

*- Wayne Dyer*

# Part 2

# THE SCIENCE

# 2

# Discovery of Negativity in Epigenetics

Let's discuss epigenetics. It turns out that according to a scientific study led by Barcelona's Centre for Genomic Regulation, and the Josep Carreras Leukaemia Research Institute, their discovery based on a study of nematode worms, is the most long-term form of the phenomenon of behavioral traits passed through our DNA, ever discovered in a living animal. (1)

The study shows that experiences from your ancestors that lived fourteen generations ago may be affecting you currently. They call it the "Transgenerational transmission of environmental information". Sounds like a song from the band Pink Floyd, but it is a very intricate part of our cellular biology. For researchers, the discovery that the brain's responses to environmental factors could be passed on through future generations via the nervous system was the "holy grail".

In basic biology, we know that we inherit genes from our parents and that they inherit genes from their parents, and so on. Our genes can change depending on how our genome expresses itself. This behavior can be affected by chemical, physical, and emotional changes in the environment. The stress that your ancestors went through was an experience added to your genome. The DNA sequence doesn't change but a layer of information is

added to our DNA sequence. This discovery is huge and explains a lot about human behavior and thought processes.

The science of epigenetics is a new field of study and these changes have already been seen in Holocaust survivors' descendants. This study of Holocaust survivors showed that in relation to other adult Jewish people of the same age, they had lower levels of cortisol, a hormone that would help the body return to normal after trauma or PTSD. (2)

The scientists also found in their study that the survivors also had lower levels of cortisol and lower levels of an enzyme that helps to break down cortisol. Scientists aren't sure why these survivors were producing less cortisol but this adaptation of the body meant that the body was allowing the liver and kidneys to maximize stores of glucose and metabolic fuels which would be a response to starvation or other threats.

A recent study that looked at the descendants of these survivors who had lower levels of cortisol just like their parents, showed that the survivors have less stress hormone that can make them more vulnerable to stress and fear. (2) On the other hand, they are producing a much higher cortisol-busting enzyme which they believe is happening in utero. If the pregnant mother has low levels of this cortisol-busting enzyme in the placenta then the pregnant mother's circulating cortisol would be too much for the fetus, so the fetus would naturally develop high enzymes to protect itself. This is such a new investigation that only time will tell how much this will affect future generations of Holocaust survivors' descendants. Humans have this ancestral layering of information on our DNA sequence but we are also geared toward a negativity bias.

*"Stay away from negative people. They have a solution for everything."*

-Albert Einstein

# 3

## The Negativity Bias

The brain has a greater sensitivity to unpleasant news. If you have noticed, the news these days is filled with negativity. It seems like the only good news that's ever aired is when the stock market or housing industry is booming. We unknowingly thrive on stories of crime, terrorism, disasters, and corruption.

There just seems to be so much more bad news than good news. This negativity bias, also known as a positive-negative asymmetry, is so automatic that there is a greater surge of electrical activity in the brain, meaning we are more influenced by bad news than good news. In other words, we feel the burn of a reprimand more powerfully than we feel the exuberance of praise.

I've been around people who watch the national news all day and conversations with those people are always a pit of bitterness and despair. Listening to the constant dismal noise of newscasters' stories of catastrophes and disasters makes me want to escape to solitude and quiet.

It can be very stressful, and the constant negative droning making me feel depressed and tired gives me insight into why stress is so harmful to the body and why so many people die of stress-related illnesses every year.

Many of the stories in the news are escalated and pumped up to make it seem like the world is always in a crisis. This is the perfect way for the media to play on the human brain's natural tendency toward negativity bias. Remember Y2K, even Time magazine put it on the cover. People set up bunkers and power generators, Y2K lawsuits were being filed and survival camps became popular. In 1999 an American made-for-television movie came out about the coming disaster. There have been eight different dates in the past nineteen years that were broadcast for the world to end. That doesn't mean there isn't a possibility of the world coming to an end, but so far we just haven't gotten our predictions right.

It does however create drama and an exciting news story that gets millions of people to turn on the tv and sell newspapers and magazines. It's one way to generate income in this capitalist society. The issue with negative news is the amount of anxiety and depression that it generates especially with seniors' mental health. According to a recent survey from *The American Psychological Association,* they found that more than half of Americans say the news causes them stress, anxiety, fatigue, and sleep loss as a result. (3)

Recent studies have also shown that pessimistic news makes audiences feel helpless. A study at The Reuters Institute for the Study of Journalism Oxford University in 2017, showed 48% of people stopped consuming news media because the news had such a negative effect on their mood, 37% said they didn't trust the content and the rest felt like there was nothing they could do about it anyway, so they stopped following the news. (4)

There is hardly ever a positively uplifting story in the news. Negative news affects people's psyches and makes audiences feel less likely to engage in solving global problems or getting involved in public debate. It can also create or even trigger PTSD. This spewing of negativity won't affect everyone but more likely it will affect those that are prone to these conditions. Negative news can still lead us to ignore the things that are working in the world and heavy news watchers can become out of sync with reality, worrying about crime even when crime rates are falling. Sean Dagan Wood, the co-founder of the Constructive Journalism Project, recently said in a TED talk that "A more positive form of journalism will not only benefit our well-being; it will engage us in society, and it will help catalyze a potential solution to the problems that we face."(5)

Research shows that there is just as much good news as bad news but ratings tend to drop when bad news is sugar-coated. A news site called the City Reporter ran an experiment for an entire day showing only good news of "sunshine, lollipops, and rainbows" according to one source, and two-thirds of their ratings dropped for the day. When life is good you don't need to listen to how good it is or read about it, it's just life as usual. We want to know the bad news so we can prepare for disaster. The mass of nerve cells in our temporal lobe which is attached to our visual and auditory channels is a sort of danger detector that is always scanning and keeping us on high alert. It's imperative for the survival of our species. This is part of the built-in negativity bias.

The negativity bias gives us the ability to weigh something that is dangerous and helps to keep us out of harm's way. It's for our survival and helps us in determining danger. This creates the potential for negativity to encompass all areas of our lives. It's hard to run away from since it's a well-developed system that makes it unavoidable to not recognize danger.

What this means is that our brains are wired with a bias toward negativity because that is what helps us survive. Let me give you an example, imagine that you are a cave dweller and you are surrounded by animals that want to eat you, harsh environments that can harm you, and food that could be poisonous, and on top of it, you have no language. What is most important to you is that you remember what things in your environment are dangerous. The more you remember these negative things the longer you will survive. It's also known as negative feedback. We remember the pain, suffering, injuries, and other negative outcomes in case they happen to us again. It's a way of preparing for the worst or not having it happen at all, if possible.

An example of negativity bias in modern times is a person who is afraid to fly because they have been choosing random negative information about flying and letting that take over their thought processes instead of getting the facts about flying. Let it be known that your chances of dying in a plane crash according to the NTSB (National Transportation Safety Board), is one in 29.4 million. (6) That's an incredibly small chance that it will happen.

Our brains are also very evolved and allow us to imagine the future. It would be great if our brains allowed us to always imagine pleasant and wonderful outcomes all the time but then if we think about that cave dweller deep in the jungle, petting that vicious lion that wants to eat you for dinner or eating a handful of beautiful poisonous berries, might not make for a very long life. So the negativity bias keeps us in survival mode and able to pass on those genes to the next generation.

Negativity bias can happen anywhere at any time and be triggered by many different things. We can see it not only in the news but at school, in the workplace, at home, and even at play. Have you ever experienced a stressed-out coworker, or a pissed-off boss or had constructive feedback that completely overshadowed any positivity you could drum up for the day? I'm sure many of you have, and most of us experience some kind of negativity daily when driving in traffic. There seems to always be one person that has lost their mind to it and has decided to risk everyone else's life on the road that day.

Most of us spend at least 8 hours a day at work so having a workplace that is light, happy, and enjoyable would be most desirable. Stress, however, creates a fight or flight response which makes the brain act quickly just like it would in a life-threatening situation. During these stressful times, we have to learn to balance our thoughts and use all parts of our brain, not just the survival part. We can do this by gaining perspective, is the situation going to hurt us? Becoming aware of what we are thinking, and gathering clarity of the situation. Then accept the negative and stressful thoughts but look at the positive sides of it, as there is always a positive side. Let the positive reside in your mind, stay with it, and allow the change to take place over time as you repeat these steps, you will become less stressed and negative.

*"I will not let anyone walk through my mind with their dirty feet."*

*-Mahatma Gandhi*

# 4

## Negativity and Cellular Aging

"Negative thoughts harm your health at the DNA level", according to Nobel Prize-winning molecular biologist Elizabeth Blackburn and health psychologist Elissa Epel, in their book *The Telomere Effect*. They explain that research shows that "Your lifestyle, social relationships, and environment all affect your genes. Even though you are born with a particular set of genes, their expression can change under the circumstances." (7)

The DNA components called Telomeres are keys to determining how fast your cells are aging. Telomeres are the end caps of the 23 pairs of chromosomes that make up our DNA. The length of our telomeres is inherited from our parents, so people can have shorter or longer telomeres from birth. One major reason your cells grow old is based on short telomeres, however, lab tests have shown they can also grow longer. This means that it is possible for aging to be accelerated or slowed down and in some aspects reversed. However, having very long telomeres have been linked to a greater risk of melanoma, lung cancer, leukemia, and brain tumors. So having telomeres in a middle range is best.

Blackburn and Epel found that those people who have "cynical hostility" or grow angry and think someone has cheated them in some way, have short telomeres and are prone to cardiovascular disease, metabolic disease, and even die at younger ages. (7)

Pessimism has also been found to shorten telomeres which again makes age-related illnesses, like cancer or heart disease progress faster, thereby increasing the chances of early death. They also theorize that ruminating over a bad situation is destructive. When you ruminate, stress stays in the body long after the reason for the stress is over. The resulting depression and anxiety make your telomeres shorter and lead to progressive cell aging.

Suppressing negative thoughts makes things even worse. This avoidance of negative thoughts and dealing with stress by sinking the bad thoughts into the deepest levels of your subconscious also makes telomeres shortened. This action tends to increase stress, not eliminate it. The best way to keep your telomeres at a healthy length is first to be mindful and more aware of your thoughts. Awareness helps keep negative thoughts in perspective, therefore allowing the more positive aspect to flourish. It's more or less the act of awareness and being in the moment, this has been shown to promote stress resilience.

Blackburn and Epel found after a study of 250, healthy, low-stress women ranging from 55-65 years old that the highest levels reported of mind wandering shortened the telomeres by around 200 pairs, which equals about four years of aging. To put this in context, a 35-year-old generally has around 7,500 base pairs and a 65-year-old has approximately 4,800 base pairs. (7) This was also the case regardless of how much stress they had in their lives. Some mind wandering can be ok but when it becomes unhealthy it can mean you are unhappy and experiencing higher levels of resting stress hormones.

They found that unhappiness played a big part in mind wandering, so instead of trying to suppress or ignore your negative thoughts, increase your mindfulness and awareness. Meditation is a great way to discover mindfulness but also finding the positive in every negative situation can also heighten awareness and lengthen telomeres.

In 2010, the first study was conducted to show that meditators have significantly higher telomerase activity than non-meditators. This was the first study to link meditation and positive psychological change with telomerase activity. Another study was conducted in 2013, led by Elizabeth Hoge, M.D., a professor of psychiatry at Harvard Medical School, compared telomere length to experienced loving-kindness meditation (LKM) practitioners with that of non-meditators. The results showed that long-time meditators had longer telomeres overall and that women meditators had significantly longer telomeres as compared to women non-meditators. (8)

These findings support mindfulness and awareness by showing meditation's positive effect on cellular aging. An increased number of studies have been conducted over the last decade reporting the positive impact meditation has on cerebral aging. While telomere length and telomerase activity constitute two different types of studies, the outcomes are consistent with the idea that meditation is protective against cellular aging.

*"Stop being afraid of what could go wrong and start being excited about what can go right."*

*-Tony Robbins*

# 5

## Positivity "Matters"

Positivity, as we can see, affects aging and brain matter. Meditation is used in studies on the length of telomeres to show the effects on cellular aging because it has been shown to reduce stress, and when we reduce stress, we automatically have a more positive outlook.

Stress triggers the fight or flight mode in the body and affects the body in several ways. Your heart speeds up, breathing gets heavier, digestion slows and glucose and fat are released to give you energy, and the inflammatory response is also activated.

These responses create physical damage to the body, but the damage is worth it when you are hunting mammoths and running from saber-toothed tigers. Since we are no longer cave dwellers and trying to escape the saber-toothed tiger, the stress triggers come from modern-day life situations.

Regular practice of meditation has been shown to increase the thickness of grey matter and neuroplasticity. Grey matter is the major component of the central nervous system which is responsible for the brain and spinal cord which controls our muscles and sensory perception such as seeing and hearing, memory, emotions, speech, decision-making, and self-control.

As we age grey matter volume in the brain decreases thus leading to memory problems and poor decision-making. Studies such as the one led by Sergio Hernandez of the Universidad de La Laguna and published in the Public Library of Science One Journal, using functional MRI results revealed that grey matter volume was larger in meditators than non-meditators across the whole brain. (9)

Neuroplasticity is the brain's ability to reorganize itself by forming new neural connections, which is the mechanism for learning and memory. It's an important benefit that allows the brain to restore old, lost connections and functions that have not been used in some time, enhance memory, and even enhance overall cognitive skills. Our brain's neuroplasticity makes it possible for us to rewire ourselves toward good when we become attuned to positive emotions over negative ones.

There are many ways to increase grey matter and improve brain function and neuroplasticity, some ways are meditation, juggling, tai chi, yoga, exercise and even playing video games. Yes, believe it or not, some studies show improvements in brain function using MRI scans on video gamers. Gamers in the studies had more grey matter and better brain connectivity. Many things reduce grey matter in your brain and the most common one is chronic stress.

Chronic stress includes prolonged emotional pressure, traumatic events, buried emotions, and even daily habits such as smoking, excessive screen time, and poor diets. These can not only affect the brain but also our cells leading to an increase in cell oxidation, also known as oxidative stress. Oxidative stress is a general rusting and breaking down of our cells. In the same way, an engine will rust, and so do our cells. And that means all the ten different cells in our body. So, as you can see, negativity can increase aging by shortening telomeres which damage DNA and increases oxidative stress, which speeds up the rusting of our cells.

This demonstrates that there are a lot of good reasons for us to increase positivity in our lives. Fostering positive psychological growth will change the way you live life and possibly help to increase longevity. Improving brain function isn't just about living a long life but a long fruitful one, where you have strengthened your cognitive abilities into a ripe old age.

Being more positive also stimulates the brain to create more happiness, love, and wisdom. It can help to create a greater sense of inner confidence and self-worth, thus leading to better relationships, whether it be in everyday relationships or relationships with loved ones. I know it's not that easy to just be more positive and we shouldn't expect that of ourselves. That's the whole premise of this book, that you can embrace your negativity and find a silver lining to every situation.

*"Always turn a negative situation into a positive."* -
*Michael Jordan*

# 6

## Yin & Yang

Yin and yang theory in Chinese medicine is the fundamental philosophy that everything is made up of yin and yang and nothing is absolute, meaning nothing is ever all yin or all yang. The same as we don't experience summer all year long, we eventually have winter and seasons in between. You can think of Yin as associated with negativity, darkness, cold, female, and death, whereas yang is associated with positivity, brightness, warmth, male, and birth. Illness is understood in Chinese medicine to be an imbalance of yin and yang.

Yin and yang are also interconnected, interdependent, and yet total opposites. They are opposites that exist within each other and are relative to each other. The yin-yang symbol is a good way to see this opposing interaction and interconnectedness.

The black represents yin and the white represents yang. The curved line symbolizes the constant change in the balance between the two, and the white circle and black circle demonstrate the existence of yin within yang and yang within yin. An easy way to understand the yin and yang theory within the human body is to understand that even though we associate estrogen with females and testosterone with males, both hormones exist within both sexes. They are never separate. As the day moves into night and night into day, yin and yang are balanced and complete a whole 24-hour day. We can also apply this to the seasons and see the interconnectedness between summer and winter as fall and the interconnectedness between winter and summer as spring. If we apply this theory to our emotions of negativity and positivity we can see a positive in every negative situation and a negative in every positive situation.

The reason this theory is so important is that it sheds light on the fact that even though we go through bad times and have crises in the world and our lives, there is always good happening at the same time.

Let me give you a current scenario. Remember back in Chapter 1 when I was telling you about feeling nervous that I might lose my job? Well, eventually I did get fired from a job that I thought could be a long-term career. The acupuncture college I worked at sold in 2020 and I had just gotten promoted to academic dean at the beginning of that year. I loved my job and worked extremely hard climbing the ladder, putting in long work hours, and even working at home to make sure that the school was compliant with accreditation. As a matter of fact, along with another colleague, I headed an extensive accreditation project that was able to get the school off of the probation it had been on for 5 consecutive years and at the same time created frameworks that put the school ahead of other acupuncture schools when it came to didactic and clinical outcomes. This was a huge accomplishment and it felt great to build up the program for our small acupuncture college to match what some of the most prestigious western medical institutions were doing regarding educational outcomes for graduate medical education.

Unfortunately, it all turned south around August of that year. Not only had Covid just hit in March of 2020 and shut down the entire state of Florida, but the people who bought the school decided that it didn't matter to them if all the tenured administrators and employees had taken the school to another level. They didn't want to pay our salaries and didn't trust us, so they fired most of us. Many others ended up quitting a year later as the ship began to sink. In all honesty, I was devastated. Not only was that my alma mater, but I loved teaching and helping students become the best acupuncture physicians they could be.

I struggled emotionally and financially and had some very dark moments. Unemployment wasn't paying the bills and I seemed to be overqualified for the jobs to which I was applying. I submitted over 50 applications and it took me 10 months before someone hired me. Then 2 months after landing that job I got diagnosed with cancer. It seemed as if things could get worse they would, and my life kept caving in on me. The point is, even though it took a long time to get a job, if I apply this yin and yang theory it would be clear that eventually there will be balance. It would just take perseverance and patience.

Applying the yin and yang perspective means there is a silver lining in everything and an opportunity to learn, evolve, adapt and grow. As the saying goes 'every cloud has a silver lining'. Fast forward to 2022, I landed a much better opportunity and long-term career working in a top-rated hospital in Sarasota as a clinic coordinator and heading the acupuncture pilot program in oncology. I can see now that this opportunity more than likely would not have happened if I hadn't been let go. This is not just a much better opportunity with better health care, better retirement, and an all-around amazing company to work for, but it's a long-term career and financial fulfillment.

You can only ride the bottom of the wave for so long before it begins to rise again. Like the stock market, life is always in flux. When life goes down, eventually it goes up and vice versa, so there is always a positive side to the negative.

*If you don't like something, change it. If you can't change it, change your attitude. - Maya Angelou*

# Part 3

## LIVING LIFE

# 7

## Terminal Cancer Diagnosis

The year 2020 had a lot of negatives for me. Covid hit hard, I lost my job, and to top it all off I was diagnosed with the rarest and most aggressive uterine carcinosarcoma with a 5-year survival rate. I had emergency surgery following a biopsy, my medical bills were exorbitant, enough to buy a small condo and I had just started a job and had to take time off right from the start of my job.

Once I had the diagnosis from the biopsy my gynecologist gave me research to read in hopes it would help me understand what I was up against. I chose not to read the papers about the type of cancer and I told her that I didn't want to know the name of it. I didn't want to give it power by naming it. I decided that I would do what needed to be done, follow the program and live whatever life I had left to its fullest.

After my emergency surgery, the pathology came back from the harvested organs and lymph nodes. This pathology was contrary to the original diagnosis and my oncologist was happy to declare that I did not have this carcinosarcoma but a very common "garden variety" endometrial adenocarcinoma. This "garden variety" cancer is the most common endometrial cancer in women with the possibility of a full "CURE". She explained that they never use the word "cure" unless a person can be NED (no evidence of disease) for 5 straight years.

I had three sessions of radiation therapy and never looked back. I went to work light duty 2 weeks after my surgery, determined to keep up my strength and get beyond this rough bump in the road. I saw beauty in life and focused my awareness on the positive aspects of this difficult time. I began to see how this yin and yang and the glass-half-empty scenario could play out if I just took the time to embrace it and become aware of it. I had been practicing these different ways of dealing with negative thoughts and unfortunate events but never realized that I was developing it as a program. It began to take shape during this difficult time and I began to lay the foundation of the PAACT Program.

I looked at every positive detail I could find in each negative circumstance. I found that it wasn't that difficult, I just had to go through the motions. It was really up to me to do the work, no one was going to do it for me. I might have cried my eyes out one day in sadness or pain but I took that time to reflect and appreciate what was right in front of me. I was always surrounded by family that loved me, friends who cared for me, and co-workers that had compassion and kindness. I especially appreciated and loved myself as only I could be responsible for my happiness and well-being.

Even more, I reflected on simple things like the trees that stood tall and strong in front of me on a walk. I would stand and look up at them and breathe them in, thanking them for their beauty and taking their strength for my own. This isn't the first time in my life that I have had this communion with trees but plants are living organisms and have a great deal of love to share with us. People and animals would not survive on this planet without plants. This may seem ridiculous to some but research has shown that trees can improve immune function and decrease stress hormones. Researchers in

Japan have researched this practice known as "forest bathing".

This Japanese practice of "forest bathing", also called *shinrin-yoku*, which means "taking in the forest atmosphere", has scientifically been proven to improve health. Qing Li, a professor at Nippon Medical School in Tokyo, measured the activity of human natural killer (NK) cells in the immune system before and after exposure to the woods. These cells provide rapid responses to viral-infected cells and respond to tumor formation, and are associated with immune system health and cancer prevention. (10)

Six months went by after my initial diagnosis and surgery when I started having some odd symptoms. I went in for a check-up and came out with a negative result from the lab pathology, but I was still having minor symptoms. After another 2 months, I decided to get another appointment with my oncologist. This time the results came back positive for the same cancer as before, endometrial carcinoma, but with some cells that looked to be aggressive. It was very small, less than one inch in diameter, and fortunately my PET scan showed that I still had no signs of metastasis to the lymph nodes or any other organs.

My oncologist explained that she was 99.9% sure this cancer was what they call a "drop metastasis" and that it either came from the original biopsy or the surgery. I was shocked! I felt great and was looking forward to my 5 years of being NED (no evidence of disease), and now I have cancer again! The oncology team decided that I would need to do 25 rounds of pelvic radiation treatments, 5 chemo treatments, and after those treatments were done, possibly more brachytherapy, which would mean 3 days of hospitalization. I took the information and decided I was going to do whatever it took to kill cancer for good and get on with my life. Since then, I have only looked forward, kept a great attitude, and embraced life with positivity despite all negative circumstances.

# Part 4

# THE PRACTICE

# 8

## Glass Half Empty

Take a minute to look at this picture. What is the first thing that comes to mind? More than likely your first thought is that the withered tree branch is going to give way and the elephant is going to fall. Perhaps you are even a little sad to think that this poor elephant is in a barren desert with no water.

It's difficult not to focus on the negative here because we are predisposed to what we think we understand and know about the situation. The bright side is overshadowed by what we see and immediately the negative thoughts are overestimated. This is called the availability heuristic or the availability bias.

Availability bias is the tendency for people to rely on information that comes readily to mind when evaluating situations or making decisions. This hampers our critical thinking and decision-making.

If we look back at the picture again, we can see that if we look at the body language of the elephant, she looks comfortable, like she is just chilling out and appreciating her surroundings. What we can't see is over the dirt mound in front of her. For all we know, she is in the Namibian desert in Africa where it meets the Atlantic Ocean and she is happily watching her family play in the water. I chose this picture because it elicits a particular emotion. Not everyone will have the same perspective of the picture but for most, the negativity bias will be a strong factor in dictating an emotional outcome.

I call this chapter "glass half empty" because depending on how you look at the glass will determine whether you feel the glass is half full or half empty. Your perception is important because this is the spark that ignites how you proceed down a path of negativity or positivity.

You have to love the highly rated Michelin star restaurant that serves you a very delicate yet very large glass of wine with the wine itself stopping the bottom 1/3rd of the glass. You look at it and think, well this is the way fine dining is done. You pay a lot for very little. The glass is half empty so you can enjoy the 5 S's of wine tasting without sloshing the wine out of your glass. To understand the terroir and characteristics of the wine you have to see, swirl, sniff, sip and savor the wine and a large glass allows the wine's chemistry to take place.

The problem is our perspective of the glass half empty. We look at it and feel sad that we have paid so much for so little and it leaves us wanting more. Perhaps not everyone has this view but most of the time perspective weighs heavily when you feel that you have overpaid for something you wanted to gain so much pleasure from.

A study done by social psychologist Alison Ledgerwood and her colleague at the Department of Psychology at UC Davis investigated how certain ways of thinking about an issue tend to get stuck in our heads. Part of the experiment was telling one group of people that a surgical procedure had a 70% success rate, to which participants gave a thumbs up, and another group that the same surgical procedure had a 30% failure rate, to which participants gave a thumbs down.

They then decided to switch things around and told the first group that they could think of it as a 30% failure rate, which participants then changed their minds and gave a thumbs down, and the second group they told them that they could think of it as a 70% success rate and unlike the first group they stuck with their initial opinion and gave a thumbs down. They then went on to conduct a second and third experiment which gave the same results. The conclusion according to their research was "that the world has a fundamental tendency to tilt toward the negative".(11)

So when we have a glass half empty, if we could see first the full part of the glass and appreciate it for how full it is and then also have the awareness that the empty part won't stay empty for long, we could apply this concept to life and create a happier, less negative life.

*"What consumes your mind controls your life." - Anonymous*

# 9

# The PAACT Program

Now that you have a better understanding of the concepts of *ReInventing Positivity*, let me show you how we can utilize this in our daily lives. You have the power to embrace the negative and find a positive in every situation. I created a program called PAACT, which stands for *Perspective, Awareness, Acceptance, Change, and Time.*

Making a PAACT with yourself has peace at its core and is a way to hold yourself accountable for finding positivity and living life to its fullest. Remember it's up to you, no one can do this work for you, you just have to get engaged and utilize this very easy program to gain success. Using the PACT Program will eventually allow you to break through the negativity bias that is deeply seated in your DNA.

**Perspective**

Let's take a look at perspective. How do you see the situation at hand? By becoming aware of what you are thinking. Ask yourself if you are being negative. If so, take a really good look at the circumstances and find a positive outcome. For example, you are at the store and have to pick up balloons for a party. You are on the cusp of being late but you realize that if you can get through the fast checkout lane, you can still make it on time. Well, you get to the fast checkout lane and a customer is holding up the line. There are 5 customers in front of you and all the other lanes are backed up as well. We can call this Murphy's Law, as anything that can go wrong will go wrong. The person in front of you starts getting upset and making comments, which then starts to stress you out even more. It's natural to feel this way, you should be stressed, I mean, you are now running late. Your perspective is negative but to change this perspective you could find a solution. Ask yourself how important it is that you get the balloons to the party on time and what will happen if you're late. You conclude that the party will still go on and you decide to go to customer service to check out. Great solution! Now you are aware that everything is ok and have accepted that you will be late but have an opportunity to make a change. Your stress level goes way down and you become at peace with the situation. Hold this positive moment in your mind for as long as you can. If you can hold it and stay with it for 15 seconds or longer, you will begin to rewire your brain. Have gratitude at that moment and feel fulfilled as this will begin to create a welcoming blissful joy inside you.

A neuroscientist, Donald Hebb first described this rewiring of the brain in 1949 with the saying " neurons that fire together, wire together". This Hebbian saying describes how pathways in the brain are formed and reinforced through repetition. The brain is malleable, not concrete, and can change in response to repetition.

The more you can implement this methodology the more it becomes a habit, and the way you begin to deal with negativity begins to change. Give yourself time and it will become a natural part of your daily life. It's important to give yourself some grace too and don't think you will make extreme changes in a day. Let yourself have emotion but also perspective, awareness, and acceptance.

Take some time to journal your experiences. Write down all the good things that happened and what you are grateful for. Write down the negatives too so that you can get perspective on finding the positive aspects. Finding positivity in a negative situation won't always be easy, but the more you do it, the more it becomes hardwired. Remember, our brains love to learn new things and every time you search for a new positive perspective you are increasing your brain's neuroplasticity and optimizing your brain's performance. That is a positive outcome!

**Awareness**

Practice being aware of your negative thoughts and the things that trigger you. Once you figure out your triggers you can prepare yourself and work through them. Again, as you work through them, hold the positive outcomes in your mind, enjoy them and be grateful.

Awareness also means you might have to pay attention to not only what you are thinking but what you are saying. It's just as important to speak with good intentions as it is to think. I'm sure many of us can think of people we have been around who do nothing but spew negativity and wallow in misery. To some people, this can be a comforting feeling and a way to get attention. Misery loves company, as the saying goes and if we allow ourselves to be miserable, we won't have to face disappointment.

Being aware of your thoughts isn't the same thing as trying to control your thoughts. You aren't intentionally pushing negative thoughts out of your mind or pretending they aren't there. That isn't good for your mental health as it puts stress on the mind and the body, creating psychological distress.

Emotional stress, like that from blocked emotions, has not only been linked to mental illness but also physical issues like heart disease, intestinal problems, headaches, insomnia, and autoimmune disorders. From a Chinese medical perspective, emotions are intimately linked to organs and our physical well-being.

Becoming aware of your thoughts means just that, paying attention to them and becoming mindful. When we pay attention we allow ourselves to experience grief, sadness, and anger but in turn, accepting the negative allows us to have space to investigate the positive.

**Acceptance**

Acceptance is important and will help you find strength, patience, peace, and confidence. Journaling your emotions is a good activity that will help you figure out changes you might make, find a positive solution, and build confidence to move on. You can also reflect on the situation as you are falling asleep and look for good facts that you can turn into positive moments. Turn off the news, read a book or listen to music or take time to allow yourself to be quiet and meditate.

Acceptance means you aren't avoiding your negative thoughts. If you fell into a hole every time you backed your car out of the driveway, chances are you would avoid it and never get anywhere. Instead, accept that there is a hole and figure out a way around it. That's the positive outlook on the situation.

It's not pleasant to experience negative emotions as the brain is designed to seek pleasure and avoid pain. Repressed negative emotions have long-term mental and physical repercussions on your well-being, so the more you can accept them the happier and healthier you will become.

**Change**

Changes will take effect over time, as you begin to become more mindful and create habits of finding positivity the happier a person you will become. Change doesn't mean that you as a person will change, you will always be you. Sigmund Freud developed the idea that we are our thoughts. The theory implies that your physical actions are a representation of your mind and vice versa. These days, psychologists, psychiatrists, and other neurological experts disagree and deny this concept. According to them, thoughts are objects of the mind, like sounds, perceptions, feelings, and ideas. So, the truth is, you are not your thoughts, thoughts do not define you.

Meditation is a good start to accepting negative thoughts and letting them go. There are many different ways to meditate, so pick the style of meditation that feels most comfortable to you and go with that. I meditate using the technique of Transcendental Meditation because I learned it over 20 years ago. Do some research into different styles and find one that best suits you.

Other methods to implementing awareness, acceptance, and change are to start a gratitude journal or take time at the family dinner to go around the table and say some of the things you are grateful for and what positive events happened that day, you can also talk about negative situations and help each other find the positives. These types of exercises will create joy, positivity, and contentment.

Sometimes changing your surroundings is a great way to allow a negative situation or thought to be accepted but not take over. The problem will still be there but if you go for a walk, ride your bike or meet up with some friends you can come back later with a fresh perspective. Have compassion and kindness for yourself as you work through some of the rough times in your life. We all create patterns and habits that are hard to break. It takes time to work through some of these barriers.

**Time**

Time is your friend. Change doesn't happen overnight and you might find yourself reverting to the same old patterns but if you are mindful and aware of this happening then you are capable of following the PAACT Program and making a breakthrough. Like

Eckhart Tolle says "Whatever you fight, you strengthen, and what you resist, persists." If you resist and try to shove negative thoughts away, or ignore them, then they will persist. Fight negative thoughts with awareness and acceptance and you will find strength, happiness, and more joy in your life. Every day your brain processes around 70,000 thoughts, so in one day you have the opportunity for a lot of practice. This in turn means you have a lot of time to make these positive changes, and face life with renewed optimism.

*"It is not the strongest of the species that survives, nor the most intelligent that survives. It is the one that is the most adaptable to change." -Charles Darwin*

# 10

## Social Connections

You are not alone, or let's just say that you don't have to be alone. What I mean is that it's important to have relationships and social connections. If you live alone or are feeling lonely, then today is the day to start connecting. Pick up your phone and text or call someone or if you don't feel up to using the phone, send an email. Only you can make a change; you are the one holding yourself back, and there are no excuses.

There is a ton of research that shows people who have good relationships and social connections are happier people. Humans are social beings and not only do interactions with others make us happier and more positive but also make us healthier. The longest study ever done on this topic started in 1938 at Harvard during the Great Depression and is still ongoing to this day. This study tracked the health of 268 sophomore males (Harvard had only male students at that time), in hopes that it would reveal clues to leading healthier and happier lives.

This study has been going on for over 80 years and established an enormous amount of data. The surprising finding in the study is how relationships have a powerful influence on our happiness and health. Taking care of your body is important but according to research, fostering good relationships leads to happiness, positivity, success, and a longer life.

When we experience bad relationships, we feel more anxious, depressed, and lonely but because social interactions are connected to our strongest emotions, when they are positive, we feel happier, calmer, and content. The studies even show that people who are lonely and in unhappy marriages have more emotional and physical pain than those who have warm relationships.

Another important aspect of having good social interactions and relationships is brain health. As Robert Waldinger professor of psychiatry at Harvard Medical School stated "Good relationships don't just protect our bodies; they protect our brains." The studies showed those with strong social support experienced less mental deterioration as they age. Loneliness, on the other hand, raises the stress hormone cortisol and increases inflammation and chronic illnesses. (12)

Perspective can also play a part in our social connections. We can feel lonely in a crowd and even in a group of family, which means it's less about just being present in a crowd and more about the relationship with the crowd. It also has nothing to do with being an introvert or extrovert but with your perspective and feeling of connectedness. Yes, even introverts can find ways to connect, whether it be in person or digitally. Any kind of positive connection counts and the more you participate in social interactions the happier you feel.

Any kind of method of interaction is important so you don't have to sit and stew about how you are going to make connections since you don't like to go anywhere or you don't have any friends. A phone or computer will suffice, though it is good to allow yourself personal contact and not always have it be virtual or digital. I don't mean you have to go to the next Christmas party to mingle but meeting a friend for coffee or a meal is great, you could even have them go for a walk with you at a park. Even small connections can make a big difference.

I am an introvert and kind of feel like I could be considered a hermit, but that's not true because I am in constant meaningful contact with my family and friends. I am an only child and never had issues being alone. I love my alone time, but I do enjoy having friends and visiting family. I am the first to tell you that I would rather stay home than go to a party. At parties, I am always that quiet person standing in the corner waiting for someone to speak to me and a part of me hopes that I don't get spoken to and I can escape the room without anyone noticing. You heard that right. I can stand in front of a classroom and teach my students without missing a beat, but I don't like starting conversations with people I don't know at a party, and I can guarantee I won't remember anyone's name. Be that as it may, there have been plenty of times when I've been the life of the party, so go figure.

Humans need social relationships to thrive and having people to count on can help us bounce back from misfortune, help us accomplish more, and feel a greater sense of purpose. This is how we are *ReInventing Positivity* by allowing ourselves to not just be a body in the crowd but to make essential connections that satisfy the social bond that is hardwired in our biology.

Making social connections not only creates positivity and fosters success but it releases oxytocin, the pleasure-inducing hormone, that improves concentration and focus. Our health greatly improves when we have social support and can decline drastically without it. Studies have shown that people get well faster during hospitalization when there are others around them recuperating from similar illnesses, versus being left alone in a private room. The same goes for people who have suffered a heart attack. Researchers found that those who had emotional support during the six months following a heart attack were three times more likely to survive. (13)

As you can see, it's just as important to have good social connections as it is to create more positivity in your life and become a more successful, happier person. Social support has as much effect on your health and life expectancy as high blood pressure, obesity, smoking, and daily exercise. (14)

# 11

## SUCCESS

Ok, it's time to wake up and smell the coffee. You can't sit there and procrastinate about starting your journey to positivity. I've shown you this easy program to practice so now it's up to you to make a PACT with yourself to obtain success and happiness. Look at your perspective on the situation, gain awareness, invite acceptance, make the changes necessary and give it time. Don't sit there and ruminate on the past and stop dwelling on the future, it won't allow you to gain success and it definitely won't invite happiness and joy into your life.

Our thoughts, actions, and language are the keys to *Reinventing Positivity* and developing success in everything we think, do, and say. Whether we are successful at work or play, the PACT Program will guide you to stop negative thought patterns by rewiring your brain for positivity. As you develop these positive thoughts you will gain more positive self-talk, and less judgment of others, and your physical actions will become more in tune with acts of kindness and respect. All of these concepts become a solution to your success.

The PACT Program is your guide to rewiring and reshaping the neural pathways in your brain. That being the case, following the steps outlined in chapter 9 of The PAACT Program will assist you in learning to adapt to your negative thoughts and using them to see the positive in your life.

As you begin to take these steps to fulfill your journey through positivity, I want you to realize that the people around you are also going to benefit. Your family, friends, and coworkers are all going to feel this illuminating energy. It's very hard not to smile at someone smiling at you. People unknowingly mimic others' behavior. It's known as the chameleon effect and it's perfectly normal behavior. If you interact with another person or people for long enough, you are bound to pick up some of their behaviors, mannerisms, facial expressions, and gestures.

Elain Hatfield in 1993 was the first to name this behavior, *The Emotional Contagion Hypothesis*. It's defined as "the tendency to automatically mimic and synchronize expressions, vocalizations, postures, and movements with those of another person's and, consequently, to converge emotionally."(15)

So the act of spreading joy is a real thing and it's contagious. You can not only create positivity and happiness in your own life but bring pure happiness and positivity into other people's lives. Happiness is the root of success.

Negativity, however, can act in the same way as positivity, flowing like waves in the ocean. Negative actions can become so turbulent that in a few minutes an angry person walking into a room can set the tone for the entire room. This ripple can become a wave and become so powerful that it takes over an entire workplace or business.

There's nothing like having to wake up and go to a job that you can't stand. Ask yourself why you can't stand the job. Write about it in your journal, and find the root cause. Is it the miserable Mary that you have to listen to all day or maybe your boss is a jerk? Whatever it is, you have the power to bring positivity to the situation just by being your happy positive self and finding a solution using the PAACT Program.

Finding positivity is not an easy task as negativity can be more powerful and it can take a lot on your part to maintain those good vibrations and not let the negative Nancy take over. The last thing you want is to spend the next 10 years of your career dreading your workplace and feeling like you missed out on a big part of your life. This will create resentment and a void and in no shape or form equals success.

As we discussed before, the more invested you are in social connections the more ability you have to spread happiness and create a ripple effect wherever you go. This in turn not only creates positivity and success but also good self-esteem and motivation.

Success comes in many forms and financial success is one small component in a vast compendium. We can enjoy the comforts of financial success but money will never be enough on its own. Warren Buffet, one of the richest men in the world, once told college students at Georgia Tech when they asked him about his definition of success that his measurement of success is love. He said basically that you can buy fancy testimonial dinners and you can buy hospital wings named after you and you can even buy sex, but you can't buy people to love you, you just have to be lovable. He said the more you give love away, the more you get. (16)

Without good health, fulfilling relationships, gratitude, kindness and love you won't be successful no matter how much money you have. These are all keys to successful living and maintaining positivity and happiness in our lives. So go on now and reinvent positivity, make it your own, embrace it, love it and spread it, for it is all in your control. You got this, just do it!

# 12

## THE PAACT PROGRAM

## JOURNAL PAGES

These pages are here for you to practice accepting your negative thoughts, and working through the PAACT Program to turn them into positivity.

Write down your thoughts or a scenario that you would like to resolve utilizing the PAACT Program:

- Perspective
- Awareness
- Acceptance
- Change
- Time

As you begin your journey, give yourself some grace and allow yourself the time to make these changes happen. Every small step is a milestone in the big picture.

I hope you enjoy a more positive life and gain the skills to *ReInventing Positivity.* As you achieve more awareness, you will begin to spread more happiness and joy which will in turn proliferate in the people around you.

**PERSPECTIVE, AWARENESS, ACCEPTANCE**

**CHANGE, AND TIME**

**BEGIN YOUR JOURNEY HERE:**

# References

1. Klosin, Adam, et al. "Transgenerational Transmission of Environmental Information in *C. Elegans*." *Science*, vol. 356, no. 6335, 2017, pp. 320–323., https://doi.org/10.1126/science.aah6412.

2. Rodriguez, Tori. "Descendants of Holocaust Survivors Have Altered Stress Hormones." *Scientific American Mind*, vol. 26, no. 2, 2015, pp. 10–10., https://doi.org/10.1038/scientificamericanmind0315-10a.

3. Heid, Markham. "Is Constantly Reading the News Bad for You?" *Time*, Time, 19 May 2020, https://time.com/5125894/is-reading-news-bad-for-you/.

4. Person, and Helen Coster. "More People Are Avoiding the News, and Trusting IT Less, Report Says." *Reuters*, Thomson Reuters, 14 June 2022, https://www.reuters.com/business/media-telecom/more-people-are-avoiding-news-trusting-it-less-report-says-2022-06-14/.

5. TEDxTalks. "How the News Is Changing for Good | Sean Dagan Wood | Tedxstpeterport." *YouTube*, YouTube, 19 Aug. 2015, https://www.youtube.com/watch?v=zK8md-7LJ.

6. *Survivability of Accidents Involving Part 121 US Air Carrier Operations: 2020 Update*, https://www.ntsb.gov/safety/data/Pages/Part121AccidentSurvivability.aspx.

7. Blackburn, Elizabeth H., and Elissa Epel. *The Telomere Effect: A Revolutionary Approach to Living Younger, Healthier, Longer*. Orion Spring, 2018.

8. Hoge, Elizabeth A., et al. "Loving-Kindness Meditation Practice Associated with Longer Telomeres in Women." *Brain, Behavior, and Immunity*, vol. 32, 2013, pp. 159–163., https://doi.org/10.1016/j.bbi.2013.04.005.

9. Hölzel, Britta K., et al. "Mindfulness Practice Leads to Increases in Regional Brain Gray Matter Density." *Psychiatry Research: Neuroimaging*, vol. 191, no. 1, 2011, pp. 36–43., https://doi.org/10.1016/j.pscychresns.2010.08.06

10. Li, Qing. "Effect of Forest Bathing Trips on Human Immune Function." *Environmental Health and Preventive Medicine*, vol. 15, no. 1, 2009, pp. 9–17., https://doi.org/10.1007/s12199-008-0068-3.

11. TEDxTalks. "Getting Stuck in the Negatives (and How to Get Unstuck) | Alison Ledgerwood | TEDxUCDavis." *YouTube*, YouTube, 22 June 2013, https://www.youtube.com/watch?v=7XFLTDQ4JMk.

12. Mineo, Liz. "Over Nearly 80 Years, Harvard Study Has Been Showing How to Live a Healthy and Happy Life." *Harvard Gazette*, Harvard Gazette, 26 Nov. 2018, https://news.harvard.edu/gazette/story/2017/04/over-nearly-80-years-harvard-study-has-been-showing-how-to-live-a-healthy-and-happy-life/.

13. Berkman, Lisa F. "Emotional Support and Survival after Myocardial Infarction." *Annals of Internal Medicine*, vol. 117, no. 12, 1992, p. 1003.

14. House, James S., et al. "Social Relationships and Health." *Science*, vol. 241, no. 4865, 1988, pp. 540–545., https://doi.org/10.1126/science.3399889.

15. Hatfield, E., Cacioppo, J. T., & Rapson, R. L. (1993). Emotional contagion. *Current directions in psychological science, 2*(3), 96-100.

16. *Warren Buffett Says Your Greatest Measure of Success at the End of Your ...* https://www.inc.com/marcel-schwantes/warren-buffett-says-it-doesnt-matter-how-rich-you-are-without-this-1-thing-your-life-is-a-disaster.html.

# About the Author

Dr. Teresa Renfroe is a primary care provider and Florida state-licensed acupuncture physician and educator. She was the academic dean and a professor at East West College of Natural Medicine and holds a doctor of acupuncture and Chinese medicine degree from the Pacific College of Oriental Medicine. In 2020, she created the PAACT Program during her unfortunate life events including the covid pandemic. This program has set the stage for her successful battle with cancer and many of life's trials and tribulations.

Dr. Renfroe lives in Sarasota with her life partner, their two children, and three furry kids. She is a clinic coordinator and head of the acupuncture program in oncology at a local hospital. She enjoys her work tremendously. In her downtime, she loves writing, kayaking, and playing music and finds solitude at the beach and in the woods.

## Urgent Plea!

## Thank You For Reading My Book!

I appreciate all of your feedback, and I love hearing what you have to say.

I need your input to make the next version of this book and my future books better.

Please leave me a helpful review on Amazon by turning the page.

**Thanks so much and here's to your success!**

**~Dr. Teresa Renfroe**

You can reach out to me at Dr.TRenfroe@gmail.com

Made in the USA
Columbia, SC
08 January 2023